Jesse Means

•

My Eyes Are Never Closed

Dedications

This book is dedicated to the following people, whom have inspired me to write these words, that you are about to read.
Our lord and Savior, The Means Family, Melitta Germany GmbH, M. Dorst, Prince Harry and Meghan Markle, Ellen DeGeneres, Paula Abdul, Lebron James, Wesley Snipes, Grand Hotel Steigenberger, Joseph Morgan,Daniel Gillies, Charles Michael Davis, Claire Holt, Riley Voelkel and Yusuf Gatewood.

A special thanks to Mrs. Mearknee Thomas for your undying love through the years. Also, Markus Schänzle and Michael Schomisch for your support.

Jesse Means

My Eyes Are Never Closed

Poems

Bibliographic Information of the German National Library
The German National Library has registered this publication
in the German National Bibliography;
detailed bibliographic information can be found online at http://dnb.d-nb.de.

© Frieling-Verlag Berlin A trademark of Frieling & Huffmann GmbH & Co. KG
Phone: 0 30 / 766 999-0 www.frieling.de

Cover illustration: Markus Schänzle 1ˢᵗ Edition 2018

ISBN (print) 978-3-8280-3452-5
ISBN (e-book) 978-3-8280-3453-2

Short Biography

Jesse Means was born as the fifth child of eight in the southern state of Alabama in Montgomery.

Nearly one year of age, Jesse lost his father to tragedy, leaving the mother to raise the family alone. Although money was always short, he graduated from High School in Lowndes County until the 11th Grade and moved to Birmingham. For a short while, he attended Alabama A&M University in Huntsville , Alabama.

Jesse studied electronics at Gilmore-Bell Vocational School in Bessemer, Alabama. Although he was a grade A student in Electronics, he decided to persue dance and loved a variety of different styles of music. He had been singing since the age of 7 and later in life became a member in the church choir. Also, he was a Public Speaker in the 4-H Club, in Lowndes County in Hayneville, Alabama for the Lowndes County Extension Services. For a number of years, he won numerous awards competing in Public Speaking contests, throughout the state.

When he attended Alabama A&M University, he majored in Sociology and English Literature, where he learned about creative writing and poetry, which later allowed him to compose lyrics.

Years later, he worked a lot of odd jobs to support his music, poetry and songwriting. He also worked in the aviation field as an operations specialist at Birmingham Shuttlesworth Airport, in Birmingham, Alabama for 12 years. Later, he moved to Germany to persue new career opportunities. Jesse always had a love for poetry and through the years, he has written about 500 songs and 300 Poems to date.

Jesse has recorded several songs and performed regularly at local hot spots and clubs with his own material and some cover-songs.

Jesse also toured in Bulgaria for a month and also in Cologne at Tanzbrunnen, and in the city of Erfurt.

Jesse currently works and lives in Germany and continues to write on a daily basis.

No Limit

In reverberation, and in druthers, your words rebellious,
we go away from;
If truth be given, have I many doubts;
In abundance the profits obtained, truth will out;
In breathing air, the human sustenance betrayed;
From the powers that be, the world appears, like
the seventh crusade;
Off limits to smoke, a taboo to drink;
Off limits to eat, and outwardly to think;
If you eat this, you will get fat;
If you smoke this, life fades to black;
Bear in mind we are all here, at the bat of an eye;
To live our lives rather than, vexing in reverse, to transmogrify;
Life begins when we decide to live it;
Without misgivings and with infinite spirit, there is no limit.

The King James Climb

In locus of Ohio, a shooting star, emerges;
In Akron, like the milky way, you hail from;
Globe-trotting, all over the universe,
to dominate;
In the game, that you play, so effortlessly, we celebrate;
A fanfare of cheers, and happiness conveyed, that
resonates; and with every ring gained, wholeheartedly, you
appreciate;
A power forward and a shooting guard, in the star sign,
of Capricorn;
A Laker beyond the game, to emulate;
In alms, from start to finish, he gives his all;
A force of admiration, in the lives of the youth;
And through his dedication, to the game, of basketball;
He's a role model and a leader to follow, in truth;
In a glimmer of light, his efforts are timeless, in the stars,
among spacetime;
And through diligence, the game that he plays, was worth
the climb.

The Honey Bees

A bear eats honey, for his love of sweets;
Trees of bees, the bear, the honey and the fear, fear in
honey bear, the bees of trees;
Taste for honey, eat the bears of trees, trees of bears, that
eat honey for taste.
Bees of will, the stings in all; all in stings, the will of bees;
To protect the colony, like violent seas; in tawny waters that
flow of haste.
Into a seed, grows silence,
in silence, a seed grows into;
A tree of honey based;
The love of nature in the wild, the growling sounds from
bear calls;
A swarm in anger, above the head; The itchy pain of foe
falls, to bees that fly are fed;
But still, the bear loves the honey, from the comb, in which
it fills;
From the pain and aches of gory wine,
fallen at the treeline, to bees that kill over time.

The Compass of Tomorrow

Like winter, your heart, is stone cold,
And for some things, the lies, that you tell; become true;
Nearly every wish, you bring about, is upside down for you;
A double faced, and practical liar, with small hands;
Your witchery, is unearthed, for a long time, that's passed;
Disastrous in the evening of score, to others who are in
distress, a victor imbued, to feed upon;
On the range of your journeys, the power that you wield,
naively, the rage, in the saddle, can kill;
The hope for the future, of the world, lies in greed;
When money is in your thoughts, a will lost, to be still;
To believe in hope, and power for better days, is not the
only thing left on this great Earth, to save;
The future of the world, begins with the compass of tomorrow,
And what you do, in life today, can eradicate, the sorrow.

Outside of my dreams

Passed a shadow, across the sky,
my need of you; must I deny.
Like passion for you, inside of me,
in the distance of my mind; felt I complete.
Seeing you near, beside my bed, feels like the first time, I
had you, inside of my head;
The dreams of walking, with you extends, my wish to stay,
will never end.
Sometimes angry and sometimes sad, for the dreams of
you; wished I
never had.
You are my equal, but belong to another; still in my heart,
love curls and smothers.
When we first met, the lies I couldn't see, but still, deep
inside, I dreamt, dreams that would never be.
It might be unnatural, but hardly what it seems, to live a life
without you, outside of my dreams.

. . . .

The Aura of Love

There's nothing amiss, with the power you annex over me,
when love's the reason;
Like a wave, that loses no time, from the sea of all seasons;
A nebula that's brisk, even in moonlight, and individually
strong, in destiny;
Only for you, that my heart beats, a concupiscent sound, of
ecstasy;
In the element of my elongated ride,
aroused in a tizzy, I feel;
You are the one, who brings forth, the Aura of Love, inside
so breathlessly;
With all of your heart, you heal the wrangle, that I endure,
day by day;
I'll be loving you, forevermore repeatedly, on the Apex, of
the sun's way.

· · · · · · · · · · · · · · · · ·

Disenchanted Life

Bewildered by fate, disenchanted life;
Abiding wounds, that twinge, like with a pruning knife;
Like a gust of wind, relinquished, from where I stand;
So earless, to the cautioning, of the hour hand;
A life abandoned, wordless, of a time to speak;
Of the memories, in the dark, with eyes so bleak;
Many Galling nights ensued, among the rubbish heap;
That environed, the phasing, of my counting sheep;
The clique, in the streets, that you thought you had;
Brought about, an unfriendliness, that finished sad;
The True colors, of the masses, that you never knew;
Opened my eyes, from the pain, had I outgrew;
Bewildered by fate, disenchanted life;
A spiritual call, from beyond, the afterlife;
The lights, a flicker in my mini suite;
enlightens, the mood of feeling incomplete.

The Scars from her Past

Lying in the womb of Genesis, waiting to conceive a new life.
Deciding for herself and for her life, but not for me, I didn't
have a chance. Quietly she listens to those who speak of me,
on her behalf, undeniably, reminded of the scars from her
past. They heard her cry at a
distance, but failed to hear my voice, for the first time in
an instant. I know nothing of her words, and she will never
know a thing about me, but the pain, I'm just a memory. I've
longed for her touch in my heart, that never was. I never
felt my heart beat, until it slowly skipped out of life and the
Genesis that remained, returned to the dust of the same.

Honey Trees

We are all trees, when we grow or outgrow, the things, we
try, to reap what we didn't sow.
But this tree, has limitless leaves, destined in the valley
of timeless dreams, to appease your tastes, for centuries.
Those who are afraid to speak, are quiet, unlike those who
are afraid to feel, turn to violence.
Those who pray for peace, can still hope to acquire it.
The prickly pear holds on to the branches, but does not
meet the needs of bees, unless you're a bear, who cares for
the bees, the honey and the trees.

A Dream Out of Touch

Even when your thoughts, are meager of me, I think of you;
If you use your eyes, and witness, how I feel, the
sincereness, of my love reveals;
That my love is blind, when I draw a blank, in the median,
of my heart and mind;
You are the treasure, that I seek, more than I, could ever admit;
Before I first, open an eye, a vision of you, is in it;
With time, I hope this dream, is not a dream, but my heart
is scarred, so very much;
So true and clearly to me, but still a dream, that's out of touch;
Like a scarecrow, in the roughhewn of the field, before the
swan song, in vie of you;
If crows be wingless, my love be remodeled, a paramount to;
Love takes time, but I feel like, its dying out, it'll be in vain,
to pass muster on a dream, that will, never ever, come about;
You're out of touch, and out of my reach, as such is life, an
eternal beseech.

Fake Love

Love was good, without the help,
Of a rendezvous;
That naturally, I thought perchance true;
Divergent to a time gone by, in the wind, be the last;
The cosmos of the gift ensnare, what my heart, innermost,
could never bear;
Like a game of marbles, inside my head, no more than I,
could ever forget;
In trundle with someone else instead, as clearly, as deceit
onsets.
To a grinding halt, we go our separate ways, to love another,
your truth ablaze.
For what I now know, and hoped inside was untrue, but
now, I despise.

Love baked Cookies

A love to bake, is pipen hot; like a batch of cookies, full
of chips than full lips; Candied arts so hard and fine; like
bodies of scones, as soft as butter.
I love to taste the cookie dough, both dark and light, the
essence of love, had I, in head;
The shape of pastry-like dough of thighs, without a few,
bakes urge to shreds. I know its good, to roll the mix, by
hand, always my love; The pins you roll, feels me up inside;
that I submit, to sky above; At night you haunt my mind
instead. But still, the sky, I know is you, loves to bake and so
I do.

Black Lives

The devastation in a time of black lives, with riddles from
the graves, of the fallen cries;
An arduous past, inherited, but endlessly, in my eyes;
A man intensely hued, and deaf to the sirens, and in the
dark, he's shortly brutalized;
For the joy of his pride, and the off the record viewing, of
his pretty penny ride;
A passer-by seizes the belongings, of an uptown beauty
queen, who's assaulted;
Spatial cueing, through the shades, of those bluebell
hillbillies;
And right down to the sillies and the shots, from those
southern big city bullies, lies the grueling, and the
menacing hounds, pursuing.
In liveliness, the deceit and jealousy of another, breaks the
trust for all, of those fallen brothers;
Instead of absoluteness, time is wasted on the drive-by, and
the blotting out, of all the others;
A million things encompasses our minds, in which, we pick
and choose, at the cost of time, in our lives
That enhances the staging, for the
world news archives.

Uptown Wesley

From bad like soles in another's shoes,
Transversely, a weary time, elapsed;
Mo' Better Blues in a New Jack way,
be on feet;
In Evanescence, you ascend above, the pain;
A reflection of the things gone by, be learned;
By virtue of, the devastation, an earthly loss, that is burned;
And like all things, you come on the scene, to entertain;
In faithfulness, and compassion you recapture your life,
once again;
Another Blade, with a newfangled impulse, as right as rain,
renowned;
On the bough of glissade, you fulfill
positively, better dreams;
In a March uptown to victory, you achieve the dreams, that
many have not yet found;
Its time to beat the drum with enduring focus ablazed and
rebound.

Change your heart

When you change your heart, you change your life;
In a world made for dreams, that come true;
It's up to you, to bring alive, and to nourish, already what,
you have inside;
What come, what may, if stones afar cross your path, to
hinder you, be allowed;
Not in the least, be compelled to dismiss, in your mind, the
challenges you prevail, with pride;
The time will come for you, to see the truth, that no
Wishing Well can bring forth, avowed;
It's up to you, so say it loud.
When you change your heart, you change your life, a
change inside cascades, into our lives, where it is made.

Gone

Cut to the quick, from the shadows in the dark,
My eyes they weep from the pain, of a broken heart;
I can't believe what goes, has gone;
A vision to enliven my eyes to see; what could have been a
hinder, that's clearly, not meant to be.
You were sired to me, as an overture, and without, your
knowledge, that I now, must endure.
You were the essence, of my life, that I breathed;
You were the sun, in the sky, on bended knee;
You were the star, that brought out,
the best in me.
You are a force of nature, that I can't reclaim;
The way you changed, my life will never be the same,
Powerless to nourish, and I, cannot sleep;
It kills and I, felt like passing on. You were the center of my
life, and now, you're gone.

Life goes On

Its hard to find the gem and the vehemence sometimes,
wittingly life looks, to be unfair, by design;
A place in life again, if fearlessness be kind,
Disenchanted about the things and the dreams you left
behind.
The albatross of murky weather, left alone in time,
Finds its way back to me, into a life that was never mine;
But life goes on, even, when you want to just scream and
shout, and
simultaneously, you feel, what you just, can't live without;
The world of postcards, spiral, oh so deathly still;
Into uncharted waters be lost, in time, that never heal,
And life goes on, difficultly as it will.

In Bold Typed Letters

If I break my back, for you, in vice-versa, I stand alone;
In darkness, becomes your character, like a dog, without a
bone;
A soul, to purge, out of my life, and out of home;
In a multitude of selfishness, on the real, to see the truth;
How people, can take advantage, and walk all over you;
In a game, like chess, to watch them fall, is what you do;
Everything for yourself, in the world, and for nobody else;
The writings on the wall, in bold typed letters, be read;
In the belt of stars, on Pegasus, the truth of you, surreal;
The stumbling blocks, you laid to waste, before my head;
Are powerless to the wisdom, in a mind, unsealed;
A friendship, you did everything to extinguish,
REVEALED.

Without blue skies

Blue Skies overwhelmingly brimming in the likeness of doves. Gliding and rejoicing from the sound of hosts above. From the sands of life, we come about, our hands in prayer raised, to seek you out. To hone your ways of glory on a gentle breeze, with the Midas Touch, your love is all we need.

When we hear his word, it resonates, the word of words, our God is great! Above and beyond, our own understanding, the plan devised, to receive his prize. Stand ready and behold, his will be done, as we prepare ourselves, for this day to come. To cast away the tides, that binds our fears, for the coming of the Lord is forever near.

Look up to the heavens, and channel your faith in the light, with anointed oil nigh, for the will of the fight. By the armor of God and the shields of faith, we praise your name for all our sakes. Without Blue Skies, from up above, the world is lost, without his love.

When We Stand Together

The crosses we bear, we carry, around with us, sometimes,
what we need, is a blanket of trust; so we deny what we feel
deeply inside,
to numb the truth of things, that we just can't hide;
A revelation of life, that many fail to see, comes with a cost,
to unleash
what sets us free.
In dreams, what we need, sometimes come alive, when we
lose all of our fear, and swallow our pride.
The sacrifices we make, sometimes holds us back, when we
allow, what we believe, to suffocate into black.
We have something special, that sets us all apart, in a world
that needs love, and an opened heart.
We need each other, in our hearts and in our minds, when
united, we stand together throughout the tests of time.
When divided we lose the whole of mankind.

From a Glance

A vision, in a time, of you and me,
Where our dreams, of love, never come about;
Long after, a discovery in our universe, our time only, goes
to three o'clock;
The possibility to undo our destiny, in a timely manner, we
respond;
To emendate, this touchy time, that is gone, from all of
mankind;
If we stood together on hope, then this outcome, would've
never taken aim;
In a world unimaginable, where our lives are, on the line;
A world, where superior beings, come touching down;
The blinkless caliber of man, not on his life, is ever the
same;
But still, he's holding on, until the hand of the clock strikes
three;
To wakeup with the chance, to leave this world and disappear;
The future unlike the past, is the greatest fear of diabolic shock;
And everything, we thought we knew, remains so obviously,
unclear;
But still I feel, like I'm losing my mind, knowing, that I'm
trapped here, in another time;
Fated to go back, before this time, can advance;
And hinder the coming, of this new world, from a glance.

Love One Another

Judging by the iridescence of your skin,
You anticipate, that you're greater, than me;
Unshrinking, like a curtain-raiser, when I didn't even, hold
my breath;
A persistant lightweight in the burrows alone;
Granted that, you look first rate, all over the map, in the
view, of a curtain call;
Ebony or Ivory, Mr. or Mrs., sapphic or buttoned-down, or a
people's person, in the absence of my eyes, a blinding light,
to stare;
What matters in the utmost, is the complexion of those,
brainworking tones;
If its left and right, may love making beat the bushes, to be
endowed, like an overstuffed chair, that never falls;
A nest egg with appeal, that I can't refute.
If your heart is benevolent, and the inward kernels, of your
noggin are not festering, there's nothing, but lastingness, for
both of us;
Just let it flow, like a beeline from the depths, of those
filament locks of hair, without a fuss;
What better fits, will not bring pressure to bear, and what's
almost better than your truth, is in love, to trust;
Granting all of this, love has no color, if you're blind, and
can't see the value of each other;
Just remember, to always, love one another.

Rather than to be Alone

I love you more and more each day,
and in the guise of, nature's grace.
A memory in reverse, of the past.
A quarrel with you, under the blanket sky, of night;
Infinitely and to the bitter end, we hold fast;
To be in love, rather than, to be alone;
In the midst of ill will, our love carries on, and the lives,
that we lived, are better known;
Endemic to you, a truth, where I belong;
It's more valuable to be with someone you love, who makes
you feel strong.
To be in love, rather than, to be alone, where love is more
than just, a sense of right and wrong.

With love inspired

When you love someone, you just love them, beyond
sensuality, be alive;
Of substance, and fair-mindedness, like an inner nexus,
fathomless beehive;
To love yourself and to love another, breathes new life,
enfold to the world;
A love that's just, like a love that's regal, adorned in hearts
impearled;
What's pure is rare, and an appetite for all, to have a love
skyrocketed, like eagles;
Just to hold your hand, and to walk outside, as royalty,
where flowers all hurled;
Blowing kisses to onlookers, far and wide, in a dance of
waltz, we twirled;
An excellent applause, for the jewel befitting acquired,
before the world, with love inspired.

If you Believe

If wings of the whistling swan, can caress the wild blue
yonder;
There's no reason to say no, to the all-knowing wonder.
On the byway of life, lofty and dense,
I give sanctuary, to my heart, in my defense;
Be timeless and believe in yourself, and have faith, and
divinity, will comfort your way, like a lock stock and barrel,
in his name.
Ingurgitate what's bitter in your soul, amass your sight,
upon the light,
to behold;
As everything that you do, comes right back to you, in
tenfold;
To seal the order, in gander beyond the things, on the
journey, that hold us back, that keeps us from living our
lives, on the right track.
Believe in yourself and remain strong, when you feel like,
the weight of the whistling swan, hinders you, from moving
on. It's all in what you believe, that wings can touch the sky,
it doesn't matter, which faces denies, if you believe.

Until my wings touch the sky

Until my wings touch the sky, there will be only you and I, standing before a time upon high. The road is long and narrow with his eyes fixed on the sparrows, but only for a chosen few. Whom could it be, could this be true? By the guidance of the seven spirits of heaven and the human race and all the glory of his saving grace, he has given you exactly what you could embrace. He has not given you the spirit of fear, but has given you the power to keep you near and complete, so that you can always remember to kneel before his feet. Step away from the things and temptations that cloud your mind and your precious time. Step out on your faith and let it guide you to the heavenly hills of everlasting saints.

Until my wings touch the sky, your might and glory is too great for man to ever deny and that's why I remain by your side.

I don't belong with you

I don't belong with you and you don't belong with me, as time passes by, your truth sets me free. In the sign of the times, praying on bended knee. We're running out of time, that only, few of us can see.

Believe what you want, its the last chance, without the rhythm, of a rhyme, it's the last time.

Who are you, on bended knee? The melancholy on the wall, closes my eyes to it all. In time, as it stands, I pay the price, for the one's, who know very little, about sacrifice.

I don't belong with you and you don't belong with me, it's time I pulled back, from the pain of tragedy. I cannot wait, I cannot wait, one day you'll understand, just when it's too late.

But now I see

The light in my eyes, was meant to be, through scars and bruises proved my destiny.

There is more to me, than what you see. Those days are gone, living with the pain of three. No April rain, or the morning dew, to look upon, blessed with the same eyes as you. In the echos of memories, I'm not alone, with the sight to see how, it all carries on. Was blind in one eye, but now I see, a time we let go, of our jealousy. You don't have to like me, I'm not here for you, in time, it will tell if, your love was true. Friends come and they go, in their own way, today you're a friend and tomorrow in the gray.

Was blind in one eye, but now I see
the people who once called themselves family.

Old Wallpaper

In addition, a revelation of nature that I, deem likely in a
sweep;
An imminent cloudburst in gander turned down, so
blatantly without a peep;
Heightened in sensitivity, be all ears, reawakened;
To the setting of sights, on the pie in the sky, are now
forsakened;
Into a fissure of emptiness, set into motion, the residue of
the spirit poisoned;
On the outside of sensation, in a twinkle, disintegrated
from enjoyment;
A faded conscience mislaid in fondness, completely erased;
To a ghastly time elapsed, emaciated like toxic waste;
To cover all bases furloughed, be it more fitting for me;
To be in control and to ward the Celestial Chi;
From an unfriendly spirit conspiring, in opposition to see;
The putrid air breathed, is lost, in a vapor;
Like a time that arrives, to remove old wallpaper;
Wherever your destiny usher's you, may you unearth the
answers in time;
But now, as a necessity, is your energy diminished from mine.

On bended knee

You're afraid to love and what could really be. Obscurely
and distant, you fall between the cracks that you cannot
see. So fearfully, you flee away from me, even when I'm
down on bended knee. The diamond ring severs the shards
of my once shattered heart. The gravity of the words,
you spoke so gracefully upon my face, lingers once more
throughout time and space. As clearly as, my mind reigns
free and awakened, the spirit within remains forever
unshakened. In my serenity, the thoughts of you drift
swiftly away, without a trace, in another time and place.
Like a wrinkle in time, the pillars of hope between us,
remains uniquely intertwined.
Time reveals the truth in all things not meant to be, even
when I'm down on bended knee.

Fighting to Belong

You controlled me with the powers that you had over me,
by keeping me sheltered and feeling selfless. You raised
your hands at me in anger, cascading the waves of my fear
of you, like a strangler. You took many years of my life away,
still I pray, that your eyes will open up for you one day.
You have left many marks upon me. You have left my skin
and my mind branded, like that of a beast. I can never be
normal, like the rest of your offsprings, you've left me torn
apart, with my eyes bleak, with terror in the dark. This is
not a birthmark, but just the scenery of a lost memory, of
the stigmata, inside of me. So effortlessly, you burned it in
my mind, on the longest highway, for a lifetime. You are not
batting on a sticky wicket, but striking wildly on your son.
You make me feel, like a Still-Born baby, fighting for a life
whilst fighting to belong.

The hungry cries

She was a mom, for a child ill-fed, the cloth of her clothes to aid. Aid to clothes, cut from the cloth, her hunger was the sound of pain;

In the stomach cries air, air of cries in the stomach. A child, that cries, is a hungry child; is still, a child hungry that cries; to luxury in a crazy world and dies; inurn in ground on hummock. The father knows, the father sees, the father sees what he knows, because food reflects water, when hollow; lay bairn in earth a child through; with chords, of music, that followed too. To pray and hope, that it all was a bad dream; led tears of the crowd in screams.

Weeping Willow

Aching arms arching anger;
Wintry words whistling wrangler;
Forever fearful feeling fingers;
Sorrow's swimming sinking strangler;
Fickle friend foregoes frenzied feelings;
Living legend loses lenthy limbs;
Holy Heaven harrowed Hazzan; freezing flurry finishes fun;
Well wishes weeping willow;
Paseo presto Palaeo's pillar;
Fickle friend foregoes fallen fury;
Leaping longer lurks little Louri;
Currents crossing conflictions confined;
Scattered souls severed spines;
Aching arms arching anger;
Tremendous troubles twisted tangled;
Flushing feelings flowing fairway;
Weeping willow whelms waterway.

It's Paula

The way you maneuver your feet, and torso on the
dancefloor, to the music beat;
With tapping steps, you tread all in all, abounding technique;
Dancing stars in a dream, with Bob Fosse and Fred Astaire;
In all that you preserve, on the stage,
your fortitude ensues hope;
An earthy coryphee that enkindles,
the lives that remain, in the wake;
A pacesetter, on the dancefloor, to admire;
An upheave that aids, to keep the weight, of the world afloat;
In allegro, her moves come alive, as love, dole out, to mankind;
A savvy individual and a nice helping, of carrot cake;
In the earsplitting sound, of the crowd outside, like giants
splashing in a pool;
and side by side in fanfare salvo, it's Paula Abdul.

Melitta

The lines are long, and my patience, wears thin,
anticipation comes nearly, to an end;
I love the way you smell, like vanilla steam, and so full of
everything, that I need;
I can barely make it to the doors, to deliver me, from the
grounds of those pinning sounds.
You can percolate for me anyway, anytime, of everyday,
with just a chance, to sip a taste of you.
In the strains of mocha, and vanilla beans, by morning light
awakened, from illucid dreams.
The lines are long, and the moment is worth the wait;
The breath of your aroma, in every sip, that I take;
There is no me, without, a cup of you,
Some days can go, irry wrong; but with a whiff of you
Melitta, I always remain strong.

. . . .

Out here

Everyday we pass lost souls, before our eyes, on the streets;
That have fallen in their lives, to the daily grind's defeat;
With nowhere to go, and nowhere to hide;
From the life once lived, trying to live to survive;
Men, women and children, so eyeless to the world, gone;
Find themselves still hanging on, to the world, they've once known;
With miles passing by, over their heads, is called a home;
On the wings of harrowed angels, be the cost, they're not alone;
Through the gloomy days of bad weather, continuously moving on;
To overcome the daily struggles, and abounding dangers of fear;
In a world living crowd, in the darkness, out here.

We're all winners

Our time is short, and our lives a glimmer;
Our minds are warped, where truth is dimmer;
Our homes and hearts, be lost in time;
Our love is made, taking chances into mind;
Our friends and family, forge memories throughout life;
Our world is abundant, in hate and in strife;
Our future could be brighter, if we all could cope;
Our world couldn't be lost, if we didn't lose our hope;
Our time is short, and our lives a glimmer, when we
overcome our differences, we're all winners.

In the midst of a Prick

By what means, be cognizant of the mislead, and the
frequently nipping of their lips; abashed in gander away;
Bear in mind, with observation, and give an audience, to
beauty or a handsome face, and the making of
those eyes; and to the rhythm, of the powers that be, a flutter;
The hands avail, a spoken gesture, in a veil of secrecy;
disguised.
Face to face, man or a woman, lanky and feeling exposed;
to a surprise;
The infallibility, to call a spade a spade, of who they are,
dismayed;
Mind your P's and Q's, and those clammy fists, by what
means, a prick, reflects;
In the moment, the truth of what has been spun; stands
erect.

Go Away

I cannot presume true, what you bring about to me;
An entity without weakness cede;
Bitterness infused amidst, a false move, in a fissure of woe,
the lies
disprove;
Loudly in anger, I orate, go away!
In a stroll over me, to succeed, you estimate;
At the end of the rainbow, as I can see, the shape of your
embodiment, worn;
And not even, on the veiny part of me, to manipulate.
Over and above, you hit the sack,
and turned out to be a chimera, like
a cover girl, you skitter, in a strange form, on davenport;
man jack.
Never a smooth, or a clandestine thought, be left;
A Judas kiss of lies and deceit, straight from the author's
heft.

On the Mount View

In Winter, Spring, Summer and Fall,
basking in the nearness of balance, with clouds, like cotton
and starry skies, so blue;
In the swiftness, of the breath of life, and in a blitz, a Vista
relaxing;
The picturesque of your warm embrace, soothes life below,
in relief, from emptiness;
Flowers blooming in the rigidness of the wild, in a call to
nature, where the Apex looms;
Beyond the horizon, from the noise below the hills, the
wisdom and proof, of God revealed;
An awakening to ingest, for some moments, in a life of peril,
consumed;
In the greenery of the strewed, a renewal of life endured;
In the chasing of moonlight, the heavenly stars a flux, in a
zoom;
Swiftly in forgetfulness, the thought of time itself, passes by;
Whilst in the memories, of the days ahead, in boom town,
secured;
The love of Winter, Spring, Summer and Fall, comes alive,
in the thickness, of human nature's call;
And on the mount view, an abounding vegetation befalls;
In relenting peace and allurement, in the surroundings of
us all.

· · · · · · · · · · · · · · · · ·

Fresh Air Clouds

A lonely bright star shimmers of hope, for the world, and sky;
Nocturnally, to nurture our ways, in harmony;
The darkness above, upon high, in silence;
In the days of yore, arise a new idea ahead, be awake;
The flocking sounds of the birds, abaft in the greenery, to
prepare;
While anticipating the shining of the sun,
Whilst phasing tallies, of mountain sheep;
A star that captures the darkness, without moonlight;
So brightly, it shines above, with the spotlight of man, in
the crowd;
And still, makes its way, back to us, in a round;
In silence of the night sky, a star blanketed in darkness,
unites;
A breezy wind, encircles my face, leaving a bouquet,
cascading in douds;
To embrace my presence, with a brisk of fresh air clouds.

In Everything you do

In adoration, I grasp at the thought, to be in love, with you;
Every now and then, like adamantine
unyielding, and convincing me, to carry on;
Whilst in dire straits, a course of action is taken, which
leads to a place, that can't be found;
In headland above, in a glance, I feel that, I'm heaven bound;
And within these walls of quintessence, an inner voice in
firmness, forges ahead;
And upon the breath of air, I know deep down that, I'm not
alone;
Upon the highest cliff, my faith in you, is forever strong;
In continuation on the journey, a joy washes over me, like a
river, that nobody knows;
If God be ingrained in the greatest, with you, he'll make a
way, that's true, in everything you do.

T.G.I.F.

Coming out of, a lengthy grindstone,
at the juncture;
But, in furlough I reminisce, on an opposite path, that's
more condign, than two days;
And for the weekend, is my projection, changeless;
Seafaring on the beaches, of the Black Sea, on the spot, in
the wind;
The essence of sea, and the vigor of sunlight, in diverse;
In nostalgia, to savor cuisines, that resonate with summer,
to never rescind;
The loudness bring about, the melodies, to beloved songs of
harmony, inside;
On an abundant course, the Mai-tais and Caipirinhas give
power, to a good time, pinned;
Going with the flow, I feel the Earth completely, in the
nether terrains, of my feet;
The days of Friday, departed and now emerges, the early
bright;
A happy charisma, to stroll on the sands of the beach, an
absolute treat;
All in all, is the weight of the world, lost into, the looming
night;
In the weeks of merriment, I lose time to reflect, on the
things, that I left;
And to finally, kick-back and release, T.G.I.F.

. . . .

A Mother's Intuition

By virtue of the daub, your limbs far-reaching apart;
To pass muster, for the forebearing of child, beget;
Intuition of the creator, a child of interest, within reach;
Through tenacity, and safekeeping, she emboldens hope;
That driving force, that's essential to your makings, without
a reason,
be learned;
Someone who knows, when something's not right, who's
needs are less, than your own;
Through sacrifice, and patience, her attributes earned;
If comfort be able, go wading safe and sound, afloat;
In the highest, when you need her, in a monsoon, you're
never alone;
In liveliness, on proving ground, she holds at bay, her escort
at all cost;
In Faux pas, to follow through in footing, be lost.

My Gift to You

My gift to you is bigger than a Christmas tree, but larger than a kiss, and in my heart of hearts it soothes all that I so greatly miss. Every year around this time, we lose someone dear to us. It is in these moments that we often take for granted that we should often trust to remember and acknowledge those, who we now have in our lives, instead of waiting for that time to pass us by. Every day is a new beginning to get what we didn't get right the first time yesterday and to remember to keep those we love and see everyday of our lives, in our hearts and in our minds, as we sometimes are color blind to these times, that we underline for another day in the sunshine. My gift to you is bigger than a Christmas tree that I will forever keep inside you see, to let you know how much you mean to me. Merry Christmas!

Twilight

Lying here above, the Milky Way at night, valiantly waiting to see the beauty of twilight. Shiny little rocks, like glitter in the sky, wishing that our dreams come to life, if we try. The hues of Saturn, unlike the Earth and the Sun, shimmers in its beauty, a new day has just begun. The beauty of cosmic forces, connects us across the sky, from comets to shooting stars, the dreams you can't deny.

To gaze upon morning light, is like the wonder of a new birth. A light through dust, shines back to us, on Earth. From the sound of the birds, the world of nature takes flight, shining so bright, in the beauty of twilight.

At Sixes and Sevens

In expectation of desire, your chance completely, a gaze;
Attached to another, link in chain, be related;
Missing from the moment at hand, and in continuation,
your words unbroken;
The materialness, of the words uttered, remained pointless;
By reason of what you, took a shine to; and amassed, than
what I let have;
Your friendliness, was not in the field of view, and at sixes
and sevens, amour, disjointed;
A fair-minded acquaintance, that you misconceived and
deliberately a call takes form;
The anger inside appointed, into the ears of the world scorn.
In the blurring of the truth, may your heart unravel;
Into a place, outside space travel.

Tried and True

In the briskness of all things possessed, and in the merciless daily grind, we mislay;

Through the inner workings, we figure out, the rapture of man, that comes about;

Exclusively, for a short time hitherto, be forthcoming, whenever, could be the last;

Its better to learn, from the lessons endured, from the gray matter of life, in the past;

The apples of our eyes, departed from this life, with skeletons in the cupboard, to find;

Like a boomerang, that's vexing to rebound, from all the pain and sorrow, left behind;

Always and forever, be credulous, and in travails, we will make it through;

And to remember the souls, who have become a part of us, in a life that's tried and true.

I do not walk alone

I do not walk alone through these Halls of Hope, I'm right where I belong. Dreaming of the days, that you will finally see his throne and realize truly that you never stood on your own. A blessing is to come, his will be done. What's hidden in darkness will soon come to light. The things that you believed you hid were out of sight. He comes to you, like a thief in the night. Greater than any storm to save you from your plight. To guide me home, I do not walk alone.

It's just Ice

When you've done all you can,
to end venality here at hand.
It's time to let you know, there are no limits to letting go.
Me too and me three, just feels like an eternity. Slowly they
free themselves from the chains of misery. Like a fragiled
soul, in the freezing cold of night, the boldly and revealing
truth, finally comes to light. Stand tall and stand strong
and be true in your intentions. Follow your heart, I know
it's hard, this too is worth the mention. It's just Ice, breaking
the silent lies of old, the future has finally come, which
rapidly unfolds, it's just ice.

Life is what you make it

Conveyed, collide, and without gentleness, into the
emptiness of a cell;
That blighted and blustered a besiege, directly, in the arms
of hell.
Hurl, head-on and hurt, pray to God, for what it's worth;
Gibbet and sent into the gallows, aghast into the beyond;
Life is what you make it, when the future appears unclear.
Life is what you make it, when you reject the bonds of fear.
Life is what you make it, like it's made of glass, so don't
break it;
Life is what you make it, when you believe it you can
achieve it.

Earth and Others

Dimensions of reality, that correlate in another place, with
our world as well as, through all time and space;
With energies that discharge, in realms uncharted by man;
Which sets into motion, an unaccustomed lifespan;
Beyond the bounds above, a theoretical mass, and a
treasure trove well-known, in our time, overpassed;
The stellar masses diversify, like that, of stellar hearts, with
a diligent breeding power, by fits and starts;
The stars in the heavens that die they come to be;
Nebulous where light is lost, like a mixed tide from the sea;
The one and a million charge, and sorrow of human life;
Is fraught with danger, in the echoing sounds of fifes,
The days ahead in time, we learn well of our mistakes;
To know exactly when, to put our foot on the brakes;
Language unites knowledge, to reach boundaries from one
to another, and worlds parallel, to the Earth and others.

More than that

I love you more than that, and I'm willing to wait;
For that reserved twinkle, with you, in umpteen dates, to
spin with you, like in a plate;
Unheard-of to be, in favor of, your ingenuity, and the
mortal part of you;
For the masses, without a stake, an impractical screw; for
that, a sentiment retained,
Enduringly bona fide, for the promise, of your hand in love
remained.
In coitus, never have I, for the sake of my sureness,
indivisible by, because the impression, you lay upon me,
defies.

The Artisan of the Stars

In the essence of human spirits, contrasting one another,
and in the haven of reflection, we cleave;
An Adam or Eve, on the outside of paramour, are hollowed
out, in the world, they weave;
Inspite of matrimony, a multitude of hearts, in a blue funk,
bereft;
The artisan of the stars, breathes life into words, with ups
and downs, in tempo, be left;
And with kindred spirits lost, throughout the ages of each
other, in a world with love and hate, composed;
Clandestine lovers found, in this life once again, through
the bonds that they forged, disclosed;
Until they reach the moon together, on common ground,
true happiness in their lives, be adrift;
What's meant to be, is written among the stars, in the
heavens above the clouds, air whiffed.

Head over Heels

To have you, and to care, for your love, awakens the
eagerness of me,
like a hand in glove;
Untouched by measure, and by crosswise, to each other our
eyes,
collided, on the day, was to none, a surprise;
Hidden, in the gray matter, of my intellect, what I felt;
That my love be alive, larger than, an asteroid belt.
Head over heels, with desire, that I knew, I could never
acquire. This treasure a difficult endeavor, in every aspect,
and without pleasure.
At no time would you know, if words be earless, how it is,
what I forgo.

With This Love

We fall in with, each other abode,
incognito to me, the chase unfolds;
Although, me and my shadow, for you, I wield;
Evoked the noteworthiness, of a kiss revealed;
And in that, led to something exquisite, unsealed;
Outwardly reluctant, a valor of love, abound; with no wager,
of our love unburdened, could be found;
If love be strong, may willfulness, be forever crowned,
We converse in a sequence, like a waltz around.
In the depths of my heart, we sway; a motif of fruition,
without suspicion;
Because of, what we have, will last by definition.

Darkness Falls

In life there is a light,
that shines so brightly in the night.
The moon keeps shining everyday,
in the moment I knew, you wouldn't say. You're not the one,
that you may seem, when darkness falls upon my dreams,
to take you far away from me.
I am the one who treats you right,
When the walls fall down, I'm there to fight.
I stood in honor of your glance,
to take you out, for one last dance.
Life was good, as it may seem, when
darkness falls upon my dreams.
There's nothing left of you behind,
the moon keeps shining all the time,
to hide the truth, of you from me,
The pain I have in misery.
I hold my head up, when I can,
there is no reason I should stand.
To be so young and ill today, breaks my heart, when you
look away.
You're not the one, that you may seem, when darkness falls
upon my dreams.

Everything that you Touch

Everything that you touch, dies with so very much.
You try so hard to be appeasing, but fail a simple task; for
you, that was never easy.
Your strength falls short, on wings of despair, you're not
about love, you just really don't care;
The web of lies, you spin daily into light, makes it
impossible, for you to ever be right;
The words of hate, that you continue to pitch, reveals the
daubing spores, of an irry fungus itch.
Everything that you touch, comes out in a fowl stench, no
quench for the thirst, of the lies that you've spent.
The sky above opens, to wings upon high,
the revealing truth of you, finally is nigh.

In His Hands

Where am I with God, am I on a different path; where are
you, when
you hear his words of praise, are you in a daze, as the word
of God quickens you, like that of a maze.
Take into heart, where am I really with God;
Am I a lost sheep, waiting on someone else to make me feel,
complete? The Lord is all that you need, like the wonder, of
air in the world, that we breathe;
We look at our lives, and we see, the sunshine, and we
dream those little dreams, as the sunsets and sunrises; But
still, we're lost in thee. The Lord will make a way, even on
your darkest days, he'll bless you,
and give you, the right words, come what may;
His love is forever, that will always, keep you safe.
So where am I with God?
In his hands, that's meant to be,
forever and ever for all eternity

End of Days

Money does not help the cries, when there's no food left, on the shelves, to buy;
In a time of a distant future, so nigh;
A world so lost in turmoil, that desperately seeks the answer;
A call from afar, to defend, what's left outside, in the cold;
Be rich or poor, in sickness and in health, a suffering unfolds;
Itching for a drink of water, unlike the food, but with the cost, of your soul;
By the guards, they look out, for who's disturbed;
With their past times of memories, all blurred;
When you fail to learn from the past,
the future of mankind fights, until their last;
And at the end of days, repeatedly we hold on to, wealth amassed.

But guess what?

I turn to you, when I'm in trouble,
when my heart is broken, I just can't focus. Pacing many
floors, and simultaneously, closing many doors and still can
never find a cure for these sores. You have become a part of
many lives, that June bug of the night, with never a worry
in my sight. You're all that I see, in the dreamy haze, of
moonlight. I turn to you, when there's nothing left to regret;
In a world with conflicting futures, that makes you want to
forget.
I turn to you, because you can never say no to me, because
in this life, I'm not where I suppose to be. I turn to you,
because you remind me, of an invincible shelf, with
unbreakable glass, drowning the sorrows of my naked
past. You are my hiding place, when I'm in Pain, like being
hooked, on a pill, that drives you willfully insane. I turn
to you, when feeling blue, so what good is a lie, when
there's nothing left but the truth? I lift my glass to toast and
extinguish the flames inside my head. When I'm sober, the
pain renews itself, and in my head, I lose my composure.
But guess what? I turn to you, because you're the answer
while I'm in torment. You fill my mind, when I look into
your eyes, like the best liquor for the moment.

. . . .

Tick-tock

When you hold my hand, and look into my eyes, tick-tock;
And everything around me materializes, to a stop;
You don't love me, like I want you to,
as an outlander with your heart, shrouded;
For what's meant to be, you run away, feeling crowded;
The choice you made, afraid to walk with me, in the here
and now, aloof;
Life waits for no one, and the time that you had, is nearly
over;
At the Altar for you I waited, but you left me, in a standing
cold shoulder;
You never showed up, by the turning, of the second hand, of
the clock;
If never in life, we should come together, eventually, our
time runs out, tick-tock.

Angel Chatter

To get a hold, of a million noumenon, I'm giving you the
green light, for the voyage, back in time;
With no blooper reels, in our sight, and may forgetfulness,
be gone;
Household names yearning, for the outlandish;
In the awareness of you, over the airwaves, an escapade of a
new day, downtown;
Things come to pass, in the flesh and in confidence, then
out-of-the-doors, into a new dominion;
For the world, we have so much to give, to last, for all, a
lifetime;
Settling the score in triumph, we leave out the need, or nod
of public opinion;
We will give the world, a new reflection, and together we'll
tear down these walls, to rescue the white diamonds, in the
rough;
Without a shimmer will to glow, until carved out, through
and through, all the grime;
The best thing about us, is seeing all of you, with smiles
upon your faces;
On the highest, be exalted, for the glory and the power, of
God's love;
The hardships, that lay before us, are left out in the cold, on
a dirty trail, of minions; who came, before, all of you, they
were partners in crime;
Billions of lives lost, and a million lives, are still, out in the
cold, we're here to turn the tables, of your fates;
By the will, from the land of the leal, and the heavenly
pearly gates.

· · · · · · · · · · · · · · · · ·

Ran out of Time

Our love has ran out of time, so quickly, like oxygen evaporating from the spaces between your thoughts in my mind. You want so much, but not from me. You turned your back in my hour of need. I thought our love had conquered all the things that you had that weren't even mine. This is a song, that I will sing to you one last time. The dreams and hopes you had were like Rays of Sunshine, until you crossed the line. Your days are over and mine have just begun. No more lies and no more tears, now that I have seen you disappear so crystal clear and out of my atmosphere. Like the drop of a dime, what I have lost, I shall again find. But our love has ran out of time.

Out of Time

Sowing the seed must be in vain, yet
all that was worn from the sanctuary of my immortal
sleeves, cinders in the memories of a sorrow's breeze.
Nothing but the rain has kept me from falling apart, and
the time of fallen leaves, has made me wither.
Something powerful has strickened my trunk, or could it be
something frightful or just the sound of thunder?
Day after day, vanishingly fewer leaves of myself are left
behind. Still standing in the wind, remembering the
moments, we touched the last time. The taste of death rears
the sap of my tears. Tormentation decays the mind that has
imprinted a strange rapport. For what passes before you is
invisible, but still alive in me. The crowd chanting along the
way, singing the words of the fallen prey. It is not the grief
that is at stake, but the pain and sorrow, that constantly
awakes. The seeds of life, seemingly goes away with time.
The burning eyes in the shadows, and the fear of the great
divine. The good, that still flourishes, from within, has not
fallen, unlike the leaves of my mind, out of sight and out of
time.

Love or Hate

We see the past, the present and the future, from a glance;
We hold our love and hate, in our minds, like a dance;
We try to rule what others, have come to believe;
We do our best to destroy, a love
we can't conceive;
We do more harm, than good
to ruin someone's day;
We forget to look, in the mirror,
and listen to hearsay;
We all know people, who say, evil things, behind our backs;
We all have witnessed, how friends,
use our time, for what they lack;
We hold the past, the present, and the future in our hands;
We all can choose, to love or hate as it stands.

Near Death

As I lay with my head, on the pillow;
I think of the days, that I've been given.
A silent cry enters my heart, while the blood, that flows
through my veins is numb.
Everything around me is calm, except for, the voice, that
speaks alone.
Memories of the good times and the bad, pass swiftly
through my mind,
When all is gone; there is no more crying.
My spirit is free, from the body of me, to be with God and
his family tree.

Past Life

A gift of love, and to be alive, with the universe, in calamity
through, a power burst, to make hay;
A reflection in absoluteness, instead of, the things, that
came about, to pass;
Completely with love in this place, a fruit preserved, in grace;
In the backbone, of my conviction, in weakness, I disembark;
To be reawakened, with so many things, all over, that I
embrace;
A badge made in communion, with many spirits, to discern;
A new compassed life remains alive, at the point, of no return;
Beyond true guidance of my past life, the one and only,
beyond all hope, laid bare;
Through the hands of God, in prayer.

My Eyes are Never Closed

I can see the darkness coming, I can hardly see the light,
at the crack of desolation, within the middle of the fight.
I can see the blood and tears, I can hear the sound at night,
the young and old of age, living in fear, of their plight.
Promenading down the street, and fell I, onto ground;
An earthly noise invades, at my feet, that can't be found.
Boom! boom! boom! The thundering sound of doom, and
loiter along the way, to fly the coop, encompassing at bay.
No food or water today, can only hope and pray.
The dust thickens in my eyes, that are never closed, from
deep inside.

Rebirth

On the epoch of existence, arises the hour at hand;
In a quickening forthcoming, illuminated I stand;
To the upper hand of life, in a sonorous reality;
That awakens the being wrapped tight, on the order of
spirituality;
Unified in sensorium, amidst the wild blue yonder so
soundly;
Like a drumfire that enkindles, a vital force inside profoundly;
Exquisitely beyond the bounds of sight, to mortal eyes shorn;
Unrobed from a dominion of fleshliness, into a rebirth adorned;
In latter-days many a moon, still holding on, imagine that;
In liveliness a soul renewed, on Heaven's Terrain, prayer mat.